PLUMBERS

PLUMBERS

ROBERT STEWART

BkMk Press
University of Missouri-Kansas City

A Target Poetry Series Book.

Financial assistance for this project has been provided by the
Missouri Arts Council, a state agency.

BkMk Press
University of Missouri-Kansas City
5101 Rockhill Road
Kansas City, Mo. 64110
www.umkc.edu/bkmk

Library of Congress Cataloging-in-Publication Data
Stewart, Robert
        Plumbers: poems.

        (A Target poetry series book)
        I. Title. II. Series.
PS3569.T469P57 1988   811'.54   88-6249
ISBN 0-933532-68-7

        ISBN 978-1-943491-08-7

This book is for my two sisters
& four brothers, in memory
of my mother and for my father,
who worked with the tools.

Acknowledgments

Some of the poems in this book appeared in the following publications: *Poetry Northwest*, "We Wake"; *Nimrod*, "Waiting for the Plumber" and "Air Chambers" (as "Risers"); *Focus/Midwest*, "Old Cars in the Stream"; *Chariton Review*, "A Flow Behind the Walls," "What It Takes to Be a Plumber," "Litany of Tools" and "Furnace Dream"; *New Letters*, "The Plumber Arrives at Three-Mile Island"; *The Spoon River Quarterly*, "Sleeping in the Forward Compartment"; *Cross-Fertilization: The Human Spirit as Place* (Spirit That Moves Us Press), "The Point Coupee Drive-In Funeral Home"; *Tar River Poetry*, "The Weatherman Says He's Sorry"; *Poetry Texas*, "Sunday Music"; *Missouri Poets Anthology* (Mid-America Press), "Keeping Up" and "Watching the Eclipse"; *Chouteau Review*, "Working with a Younger Man" and "My Sicilian Grandma"; *Above The Thunder* (Kansas City Association of Mental Health), "To My Mother: A New Line of Credit." Some of the poems also appeared in two chapbooks: *Taking Leave* (1977) and *Rescue Mission* (1983), both from Raindust Press, Independence, Mo.

The author wants to thank Cynthia Beard for production and design of this edition, Ben Furnish for editorial help, both at BkMk Press, and proofreaders for this paperback edition, including Nicole Dorsey, McKensie Callahan, and Andrea Wall.

Finally, the author extends deep gratitude to his wife, Lisa Dawes Stewart, son, Benjamin Elliott Stewart, and grandson, Robert Balice Stewart, who continue to support and inspire this work.

Contents

III.

ROUGHING IN

Like Dante's fallen lovers
Paolo and Francesca,
the plumber seeks perpetual union.

Where cast iron's lowered
on shoulders of apprentices,
pitch rubs off
on the right side of their faces—
a procession of one-sided men
toward slope and sump.

Below slightest wind, the plumber
cradles a chalice of hot lead,
the outward sign
of yellow smoke spreading

where spadefuls of wet clay
lie on their backs, the long
Our Father beads of Italian laborers.

Water lapses into a single
way of life,
spiraling into circles
of good works and waste

where the life of this world
cures under concrete—
epistles in vulgate,
the cloistered credo
of disposal and redemption.

I.

Saint Joseph, meanwhile, rubbed away the cold
beside the fire and saddled up the ass
and put his tools away for a long time.

—Giuseppe Belli,
from "The Letter"

BREATHING EXERCISES

for M.A.

Each night I time contractions
in a practice of the pain this child will use;
you would not know without me
when discomfort comes and goes.

Contraction begins, I say, and you exhale
deliberate slow-chest breathing, focus
on whatever dream you use to monitor
crisis and hope. Cleansing breath.

My second hand relentless
as the progress of pain, an ordeal
I hand you gently and release
the way I'd always hoped our life would be together.

I ease us with my watch into transition,
that stage that only seems prolonged
when contractions peak on top of one another
and everything we planned digresses.

You pant-blow in simulation of what
you believe will be the worst time
this child of ours will bring us.
Contraction ends. Cleansing breath, I say,

and I wonder if I will always stand
at your head and time with certainty
when we will once again be close
even in each others' arms.

The watch beside the bed collects
contractions as we sleep, like weights
we never knew to lift, a great pressure
on a tenderness I can't control.

TO MY MOTHER:
A NEW LINE OF CREDIT

I remember the Chippendale dinette
you kept polished till the twins came.
You surrendered the legs first
then the whole top and then
we moved it to the basement.
Porcelain knickknacks
on the corner cabinet disappeared
with each new kid. I remember
the large mirror with a painted flamingo
where the parakeet began to perch
and turned the backing white.
A golf ball or something took off
the flamingo's leg.
Each time you screamed
we thought you were angry.
I remember the white-haired lady
who sold cosmetics door to door.
On our couch, she said, God had a special place
waiting for mothers. I was jealous
of your place.

SITTING DOWN TO EAT

in memory of Lena

Long after I answered her call,
tomato sauce erupting, she held
a meatball on the end of the fork
as if I should eat quickly
and surely before it split
and the world came to an end.

In that day, she sprinkled cheese
with her fingers over our plates;
we children lowered our faces,
inhaling noodles; red specks
scattered on our shirts
no matter how tightly she tucked
the plate under our chins.

Instead of that sacrament of pasta,
I wanted to move against the rail
at Ellis Island, to see how
she looked, arriving kitchenless,
intent someday to travel back
by boat, of course, letting
new wine sit beside the ringer.

When she would say to me,
I can tell you so many stories,
I knew how she just missed sailing
the *Andrea Doria*, how the pieces
of one cousin washed with the rain
in a Chicago sewer, how salt swirls
behind the ships that come and go.

Always, my eyes fixed
on steam rising from the sauce:

Why are we here? They have
TVs and fruit and gold back there;
children stay innocent
all their lives, and my cousins
understand the language
of their parents' parents.

Yet, looking up from the plate,
I remember her ordering me to enjoy
so many stories . . .
and the end, it never comes.

THE BELL COLLECTION

for my mother

Sometimes it seemed we'd given everything
those holy birthdays, Christmases,
so we were grateful for the bells

cluttering the hutch: glass (some Lenox),
glass (some Waterford), brass, wood,
China, discreet angels with clappers

in their skirts, and one fabric bell
like a mute crying in a dream.

Kids and grandkids returning
through Stuckey's with bells
from Tennessee, New Orleans, garlanded

like the beads of those Dominican nuns
we could hear jingling around any corner.

In their rooms, they, too, kept the sound
of bells— fifteen decades
of Waterford glass hanging in their windows.

Tonight, you phone me about the illness
that lays one arm helpless, throbbing
fifty Our Fathers every minute of your life.

I dangle on the end of the line,
another clatter added each time
we did not know what else to give.

MY SICILIAN GRANDMA

My Sicilian grandma considered it
a sin not to be afraid of storms,
so even at a slight darkening of sky
she'd see her way to our basement—
southwest corner—beads flooding
our fingers. As long as it was God-made
she feared it, birth and death alike,
for in babies she said faded a vision
of angels and glorious light,
like the sun in her little village
so rare under her father's wide
hat and bandana.
            Once in the calm after,
we drove to a place called "tornado alley"—
a tornado had touched down—
basements lay open like public
confessions in the piazza
and my grandmother, keeping us kids
quiet in the back seat murmured
"Madonna mia, Madonna mia."
We never understood that helpless
tone a worried saint can chant,
but nothing could set
her husky voice to prayer
like a God who gets our attention
from time to time
            with a good crack.

VISITATION

Below the crib window
the last garden of years
of gardens brightens
like a mobile turning
with the slope, where,
close to the city,
a trench empties the house,
sogs the bottom quarter.

My son's steps are a dream.
The old cow lowing
in the barn, long gone,
wandered out to where
the interstate cut her down;
a tractor-trailer jams
for the hill, and sitting
hens whiten into smoke.

This is what comes of waiting
long for a child. The world
returns under cracking limbs
of an apple we've lost
the name for. The old man,
down to a whisper, says,
Green when they're ripe,
that's the kind they are.

NEWS OF LOCAL MOURNING

Boatloads of refugees wallow
in the waters on our street.
As each vessel bows-up, sinks,
the men of my family cast off,
looking for survivors.

The men of my family show up
among the dispositions
of the city: a union brother, 53;
the butcher at Buttenhoff's market,
boarded up. No matter how early,

my father has taken his suit
and the car, perhaps a brother.
The first time he woke me,
for a relative, he said, it's time
I found my way to those

swaying with their losses.
They'll all want to shake your hand,
he said, make it firm,
let them feel you there
on the dry end of their lines.

WATCHING THE ECLIPSE

It's easy to get confused.
Mary Ann steps outside and looks
directly into the sun

and becomes a saint, from whom
we want to learn about afterlife,
visions we have not yet come to.

All she remembers is bright light
and then she looked away,
as if from temptation, or grace,

or a prophecy of the loss of her eyes,
as if all we deserve is a pin-hole
view of the universe.

Mary Ann closes her eyes and visions
of the perfect corona glow
on the inside of her eyelids.

It's easy to bow down and worship
the sun, or effigies of guardian angels
shielding us from sin

as the shadow passes across itself
like a thunderhead over the mountains.
Step to one side, and it's gone.

If we were on the moon or in our own
dream of understanding heaven,
perhaps a leaf would turn away from light—

Daybreak could be taken or ignored
as any other article of faith,
and we would look directly into ourselves.

THE EFFECTIVE BROCHURE

upon buying a whole-house fan

The world inhales a long time.
Turn your bed to the window
where air journeys inward. The sounds

of shots from the flat next door
lie low beneath the rush of air.
For a while, mute love is best.

Gather your family inside
the effective perimeter of the fan:
Multiply the length of tree limbs

over the house, times the number
of First Fridays fasting for sin.
You have to help cooling along.

Most households generate heat
that will not exhaust on its own—
Set in vents for those sleepless

nights, the guilt in a glass of water
offered your son. Shutters open, turbine
spins and displaces what the river holds

that will not cleanse or sustain.
Now, turn on the whole-house fan;
air rushes into dreams of a world

that inhales a long time.
Behind the deep breath of night,
your family cools in sleep.

CATECHISM OF THE SNOW

Nuns tried to convince me.
That was their way.
I denied them even the truths of
science, the symmetry of snowflakes,
water rising or the living sponge.
Our bodies had begun to thaw
and a nun was a blizzard
of cloth, a chatter of beads.
One told me to rub the depth
of ice on my black shoes,
the May Day procession, after all,
my biggest date.

Later, when the wind began
again, my two-year-old son's
footprints filled in streetlight.
Snow covered everything,
like the philosopher's three great
questions: What can I know?
What should I do? What may I hope?
Ten-million-to-the-tenth-power
souls drifted to a corner of my yard.
My son's shadow bent
across the drifts in prayer, and snow
held his body to itself.

STARTING SEEDS INSIDE

Take your average sunny window,
one that makes your apartment bearable.
If you must, you can supplement

with any full-spectrum grow light:
if your life has narrowed,
dropped some reds and blues.

Full-grown plants need cool
soil and full light,
seedlings just the opposite.

Start them on a radiator cover
or buy a simple heating cable
from any lawn and garden center.

Provide a sterile growing medium,
one almost without noise or odor,
like any place you can live the way you want.

When the plant has sprouted true leaves,
move it to its own container
in light you provide of your own means.

THE GOLD CROSS

A gold cross rests
against the chest
of a beautiful woman,
one whom I would almost
die for; it dangles
as she bends to speak
of her latest lover,
swings across her skin
like a lantern far out
on the water. Gold:
as though it were other
than an instrument of torture
where I would love
to spread my own arms.
Would she wear a gold
electric chair
or strap to her hair
a gold cruise missile
like a barrette,
its features machined
to a soothing shine?
My grandmother's crucifix,
brought from the old country,
gleamed with blood
on sacred wounds: palms,
side, feet, and the
burning heart. In bed,
the old woman whispered
a prayer that always ended
world without end,
as if our own salvation
were precious and hanging
by a thin chain of passion
above our hearts.

SLEEPING IN THE
FORWARD COMPARTMENT

I look up through the hatch
at stars, lake bright
and sniff the cool air.

The underside of the bow deck
inches off my chest. You move,
we roll on our own waves.

When the lights go out mosquitoes
forget us, water cushions
whatever dreams we have not baked off.

Listen, I think we are this close
and trapped: miniature
as the cabin sink and cabinets

buoyant
as something you said in your sleep,
the sound
of a water bird, far off.

II.

The water's . . . sweetness was born
of the walk under the stars, the song
of the pulley, the effort of my arms.

—Antoine de Saint-Exupéry,
The Little Prince

A FLOW BEHIND THE WALLS

This is the truth I grew up with.
In making the lead connection, a plumber
would cut the pipe square,
shave, candle and tin the end,
wipe a smooth silver muscle
of lead around the joint.

There is that flow that generates flow,
the kind of life a plumber primes
when he comes home from the shop, sons
and grandsons who take on the tools
like a language we learn without even studying—
the syntax of caulking iron and running rope,
long sentences of fittings that hold
their own clear sense.

For every plumber who shows up in your basement
there are sons at home, the flux that holds,
the kind of value you never see.

And I think of my father, his plumb line and level,
and the day he took me with him to the job,
a whole story of right angles and parallel lines
crafted to a logic you could follow in the dark.

But today I work in a friend's basement
on the distance between tub drain and trap,
from brass to lead and I want to know
not how a plumber would do it
but how I, after all this time away,
can make the connection.

All the rain that has not even fallen
leans over the clouds to watch me work,
as though here, someday, those drops will gather
and hold their reunion in the wild basement air.

WAITING FOR THE PLUMBER

Things seldom leak
where they drip.

A thin layer of water
may disguise itself as chrome
or travel the patterns of wallpaper
into your bed at night.

Perhaps a flashing has come loose
on the roof
or war has broken out
on the other side of the world;
transgressions start long before
they come through the wall.

Just get a pan
till the plumber arrives.

There are women, too, whose lives
seep out
into their children
almost overnight
yet you cannot find the breaches of love
in their eyes.

This, too, is a plumber's nightmare.

The simplest gestures may baffle
as soon as they leave our hands:
The congressman on his way to prison
says he will wear his conviction
"like a badge of honor."

You know the corrosion
lies far back in the plumbing

where elbows, Ts and Ys
can turn us around, unable
to tell the source from the ends,
where the water itself begins
making false statements.

BOSS TOLD ME

shake hands with that shovel
dig manholes straight and clean
take gloves off patching sewers
while rubbers and corn flow
between my legs, boss told me
elbows and assholes are all
he wants to see, water bugs
covering the inside of manholes
like strangely moving vinyl,
boss said, don't let them get on ya,
boss'd cement your feet
if you didn't keep movin, tell you
he was twice your age and twice as good
blow his nose on the ground
during lunch, told me my back
was all he was payin for,
take good care of it.

POURING LEAD

All the precautions do no good:
the ladle warming near the flame,
lead cakes kept high out of mud,
tools wiped clean and dry.

As it edges around the hub, sealing,
searching out crevices
it might hit the slightest dampness
and blow the fitting right off the bell.

This is the kind of metal
you live with for a long time,
gritty, dauntless in the last
light of the plumber's furnace,

but for a while even lead has flow,
a molten youth that explodes when wet,
and some can land in your pocket,
burn through to your chest, and harden.

AIR CHAMBERS

Crows scream in the plumbing
every time they are pushed from their perches.

They pass through the pipes
like a clot you can trace
if your equipment is that sensitive.

Consider the conduct of a water system
contained
and under pressure

like a man so single-minded he swears when he works,
yet wipes each solder joint smooth
and shiny as chrome on finish.

It's something every plumber tells his son.

Birds are going to fall
through every universe;
there are lovers you do not mean to leave

but those small dead ends
that rise among the plumbing
keep the pipes from trembling or knocking
out of control.

Perhaps your plumbing has groaned in the walls
from a toilet flushing, or some oblivion
more difficult to trace.

You sit up in bed at the sound
of an intruder,
something circling in the arteries

or a valve opening,
another pause in the pressure.

KEEPING UP

for Joe

My foreman with the sewer district
took his breaks reading philosophy
in the crew shed, told me the ultimate reality
of this crew is monistic: You have to keep up.
In the shed you could contemplate Kant—
Is metaphysics possible?
But on the street you hang to the jackhammer,
break through all the possibilities of pavement
without trying to separate great ideas from bad:
the reductionism of contemporary oil asphalt,
to the verification of Descartes and Hobbes—
the poured concrete of hardhearted rationalists—
down to the cobblestone of romantic St. Louis
when kids at Belleview School used to recite
the "Intimations Ode," and the stages of their lives
shed each visionary gleam, broke in blocks
red as the day my immigrant uncle helped lay them
across DeBaliviere, past the Italian groceries,
in the days when I was yet an unborn soul.
Joe said cut and crumb that hole
till the top of your head grows dark
and each shovelful of dirt comes steadily
as premises of life you simply count on;
you'll find yourself standing in the deepest
thought you need. Now dig.

THE PLUMBER'D LIKE TO TEACH
THE WORLD TO KEGEL

First, understand Kegel's exercise:
Contract the muscles that could stop
urination, as if the phone were to ring
and you had to know the worst.

Such knowledge strengthens the perineum,
the whole pelvic floor, and no one
will even know you're doing it.
Practice Kegels at parties or reading

the scariest headlines of the morning,
an isometric of squinting up at yourself—
prepares you for days when the child-
like in us might even irrigate

the trough of a pew. I remember
McNamara, the plumber foreman,
as he climbed into the ditch each morning
while the sewer was still dry and clean

as we like to imagine our own deep plumbing,
before tidy households up the hill
took leave at once of those obligations
we think will never come to light.

McNamara cussed the morning and prayed
to teach the world to Kegel, to contract
and monitor, to measure and to know
somewhere down the line

where flushes mount each other in a wave,
a plumber might be working, or worse,
an apprentice like myself, unsuspecting as anyone
who lives and works where some have lost control.

THE PLUMBER ARRIVES
AT THREE-MILE ISLAND

A plumber's price is high because he uses
equipment that can channel what diffuses—
since heavy duty's standard on some jobs,
and augers, threaders, clamps and come-alongs
can bring our flooded dreams another turn.

Unless a plumber has somewhere to stand
he'll wade right in among the toilet fish
and fumble with the break below the wastes,
among those places we will not admit,
where all our bright ideas turn to shit.
But now the whole trade's dirty—used to be
just septic tanks and sewers; it used to be

a plumber always had a place to wash
when he was through to tally up the costs.

FURNACE DREAM

The first thing you notice,
bubbles float off a seam
of black pipe, union joint
or street ell, a nudge
of gas into the fire,
slow as snow. The plumber
squints into the nightmare
and begins to disassemble.

One thing you remember,
a small pilot at the end
like an index finger
reaching to touch a red
Christmas ornament, your son
coming down to his first tree,
so you check the valve
settings, control the flame.

Before you turn gas back on
it had better be right;
you watch from the porch
while your only son runs
into the burners, the secret
passages where heat drifts
into all rooms; you say,
just so much heat, no more.

The plumber controls the air
we breathe; a ferrule secures
another compression joint, just
as you were raised to believe,
though sometimes a bubble floats
off a seam, and the fragments
of dreams lie in the house
like sparks off a welding arc.

LITANY OF TOOLS

The striker snaps
its own ambition
onto metal

as the plumber's furnace
exhales
one last breath,

and my infant son's
eyes light brighter
each day to the world.

Melting lead, each blast
scowls any notion
of our solidity

and I, apprentice,
unwrap the plumb bob
from its string

along a line soil pipe
can be cast—
iron, cut by cold

chisel or chain ratchet,
given to lead, ladle,
given to labor,

caulked. Every family
hands down the tools
it needs to live by,

worn as long-held
convictions:
What we love survives.

Generations stretch
along this folding rule
given to me then

extended, as if each
section were greater
than the one before,

and my son reaches
to feel my face,
taking it in his hands.

GOODBYE NOTE TO TED

In Jefferson County, they had us
put in water,
              yet no sewers.
We tried to tell them
septic tanks and cesspools
wouldn't hold

not as though you could pull
back the lid on the cistern
and learn your own limits.

Nature and plumbing
have their own ways
              of getting clean,
sometimes by being still,
sometimes by clearing out.

In Jefferson County, Ted,
you wanted just to hold
the farm and spring your wife's
parents drank from

but the landfill across the highway
sank, and one morning
your spring
              ran black,
too much solution
among the topography.

On the news that night
you tried to tell them how
you had it as a plumber:

Things naturally seek their out.

But you choked and stuttered
like any set of impulses
in the wrong medium.

You could not live that way—
It came across.
Now, like the sink holes
around Jefferson County,
there's just a place
where you were.

WORKING WITH A YOUNGER MAN

He lifts and holds, hesitates and looks
for a place to set down the box.
In the bending of his back

I see the distance I have moved—
the first job I ever had,
lugging sacks of sand up a gangway.

I was youngest then, the one watched
by old men grinning in their rhythm
of lift and blow.

Now I take hold firmly on the stairs,
each step a lungful,
back straight to hold

some truth tightly in my chest.
I cannot speak randomly
or give away my sandwiches at lunch.

Though the heaviest boxes wrestle
in my arms and urge
Hurry up every chance you get,

I brace against a memory
of when I learned how to work—
with the old men,

their wheelbarrows, shovels, sand;
and I, trying to keep up on a hot day
with those much weaker than me.

WHAT IT TAKES TO BE A PLUMBER

Remember this first:
"Shit don't flow uphill."

In the crawl spaces sometimes
a flashlight will drop and go out;

steam winds toward the roof vent
or another child moves to Phoenix.

Think your way through the dark
half story
between ten and eleven, a jungle-
gym of pipes that sweat and drip

where, years ago, your father may have
drunk Stag Beer
among the welding flares
and become a master.

Look down now and then
at your boots
or water will rise and fill them.

Look up at the clay walls of the ditch
or they'll lean in too far,
as though trying to watch you work.

Spectators can be dangerous,
like an apprentice who trips on the tools
or follows you after work
to the taverns where you're known.

Sometimes in tenements, garbage
cascades frozen from disposals
or yields in summer

so full of grease
maggots have eaten off all the chrome.

People live like that,
you learn as a plumber
crawling into the spaces they hide.

So make sure the line you fix
angles into the earth, half a bubble or so.
Almost like the quiet flow,
you were never there.
Then you're gone.

III.

*"When I'm with somebody that's corny,
I always act corny, too."*

—J.D. Salinger,
The Catcher in the Rye

WE WAKE

Red lights beat at our curtains,
the inarticulate police radio . . .

Overhead rotors and searchlight
circle the yard, the quiet houses.

We watch from our bedroom for shadows
trying to escape over the frozen tomato vines

or huddled, perhaps, on the side porch
out of the spotlight's view.

It is just a small boy
barefoot on the icy pavement
with less time on his own than he knew.

Suddenly, no light.
Our ceiling clears like fresh water.

A few crows return to the large elms
they had abandoned.

FOSSILS INDICATE UPRIGHT POSTURE

Precedented by a single footprint
almost four million years ago,
pressure built against the earth
in the balls of our feet.

Almost the way we search today
among fossils for fuel—
where volcanoes, shale and flatland
consume themselves beneath us—

scientists calculate the weight
and propulsion forces we, then,
mere hominids in the scale of life,
placed upon this fragile ground.

We strain to look ahead now
20 years, when lightning won't
begin to cleanse this atmosphere
& there's something of an imprint in the air

and farmers cleanse their fields
of grasshoppers, nematodes, aphids,
with something gentle as a spray
and residues that disappear, they say.

We infra-red from satellites
safe beyond the ozone, label ourselves
biped and look beyond the fossil bones
of Africa, the footprints of Tanzania,

and if we go back far enough: creation.
Even if you believe in evolution,
the priest said, there came that moment
when God gave us soul, a heritage

of walking upright with certain
pressure patterns upon this land
that measure what we were
and ways that we have grown.

The heaviest impressions show up
black as the world
before any steps were taken
for which we need atone.

OLD CARS IN THE STREAM

The Black River circulates
through radiators, cracked hoses,
over fins, taking
now and then a chrome part,
flipping it along the rocks
where, they say, trout lie
big as headlights.

THE WEATHERMAN SAYS HE'S SORRY

He hangs his head, says he's
doing the best he can

what with Kansas passing on air
still warm with the smell of wheat

and all those farm boys
working behind their hay balers.

He can't explain the frontal system
that rose like a tidal wave

after a hay truck near Colby
leaned too far, toward evening.

Now old friends ring us up, drunk,
as though fallen apart in the field.

We listen for a pattern,
but they're gone quick as a squall

or child who's taken to getting high
or spring air trying to clean itself

and the weatherman never seems to argue
over what is predictable and what is not.

The smell of sweat blows in from the west
like prices we have come to pay,

and we blame anyone who'll say,
Sorry, it's all my fault.

EXTRA STRENGTH

It's something like prayer.
The medicine supposed to relieve
suffering, kills you.
Medical examiners say only
a batch or two were tainted
or *laced*, as though a quaint
Victorian had painted on them
miniatures of fauna, flora.
When we look beyond
along the river, some appear
chunky and some powdery,
or hover in the firmament
until one aspersion or another
rains our strongest defenses.
It certainly seems like prayer.
Neighbors gather on the front lawn
to shake their aprons in the wind
as an incantation of chemicals
enters the distribution chain
and someone remedies the remedies
and leaves us with nothing
but prayer, after all this time.
Place it directly on the throbbing
tooth, or under the tongue
or crushed in a spoon for a child
and let it dissolve there.

FREEING THE HOSTAGES

I.

A congregation of soldiers, clerks,
spies and one boy from Krakow,
gather in the compound
to be transported back to faith,
as a Navy RH 53 copter hovers
over the hill, where any well-oiled
machine can be Christ.

As in 1968 when the crew of the ship *Pueblo*
showed up in my barracks, rescued,
towels around the thin freedom
of their waists, the way Christ, too,
must have looked around for a shower—
Easter clearly has crowd appeal.
We asked how it felt to be saved
and to be lost, when no one
could defend their borders.

II.

We hear now of the dictator
who told three couples
the only way to save themselves
was to make love on the ground
while he and his soldiers
gathered around: The men thrashed
limply among the rifles.

Finally, the generals said it best:
Never call off a rescue mission—
you simply go in with what you've got.
After the hardest times—Good Fridays
scratched into the walls of a cell—

we create our own salvation
by showing up to be rescued.

The women, after awhile,
rose up from the dust. And the soldiers,
it is said, shot them all in the back,
while the horror of my own life
is that I sit here in my living room
and take it.

SUNDAY MUSIC

Driving my Opel, listening
to the ninety-thousand-mile engine
still solid, quiet, clean—
I let it wind out a little.

WBA radio is visiting the '60s.
Elvis just got out of the Army;
so did Johnny Tillotson but
nobody cared.

Too young to drive then, I used
to ride in my cousin's '48 Dodge,
elbow on the window ledge, fingers
gripped over the rain gutter.

He got scratch from every stop.
This Sunday, my wife and I
look for marigolds, then
they play "Poetry in Motion."

My ninety-thousand-mile engine
seems to want half a chance.
I drop it down to third,
"let the little girl dance."

THE POINT COUPEE DRIVE-IN
FUNERAL HOME

Now, this picture window,
a dead man resting in peace,
    friends
who "didn't have time to dress"
sign the register through their car window.
"Ella and John" drove by,
idled three minutes
left you there like exhaust;
    some
came through on a rolling stop
as though slowing at an intersection;
    some
just honked from the road.

TAKING LEAVE

I saw Mike Bibb come home
emergency leave, married
with one day's notice.
I saw Copithorne's
practical mind crack,
married two days
before reporting to Boise.
I saw Kalicak in a '53 Buick
take his girl,
in labor through Arizona,
to San Diego, his home port.
I saw them married in Vegas.
I saw Schroeder and Janet
leave for Anchorage,
a new way to serve.
I saw the sky burn over
oil tankers coming in
half the crew jumping
at Point Loma.
I saw them on the pier
just before leave
trying not to let on,
wanting Kon Tiki and one
more night in Subic
but drawing for stateside
instead, part-time work at Sears.
I saw apartments on the beach.
I saw them put a few bucks away.

EPILOGUE FOR DAVID

(The Bubble Boy)

When my son was born, I thought of
rushing him into a bubble like yours.

Newsreels bounced you around pretty good
in short pants, long socks, the smile

of any kid getting lots of attention.
All you needed was a long, neck scarf

like the Little Prince from planet B-612,
a planet scarcely bigger than himself.

The day my son was born, snow wobbled
large wet flakes past the window

like visitors in a hurry
to touch the earth.

Newsreels say you wanted just to feel
grass between your toes—

It doesn't sound like a fatal wish.
Yet I wrapped my own son in giant

baobab arms, to hold him off sandy ground
where another Little Prince touched down

and fell gently as a tree falls.
There was hardly a sound.

MISSOURI TOWN

for Dennis & Anita

This small flint and charred cloth
flaring briefly till the blacksmith
drops and steps to save his work

the whole shop, barn, wood shed, coal house
numbered and brought down from La Plata,
all this preserved so well

a town resembling 1855 even the cock
with his backwoods accent stands guard
on walk number twenty-two, piece 7k.

I think perhaps they had more mud
or left the excess down by the Little Blue
and weeds, too, chiggers and grasshoppers.

Together after so many years,
our friendship turns out finer than we knew.
Could we have done this all in letters?

It's amazing this flint sparks at all,
as we scratch around for something brittle
that flares up quickly and is gone.

THE EPILEPTIC

for Butch M.

The last time you spoke to me you threatened
to sit on my chest, you,
the fattest kid in class.

Today you come toward me still
because you know I won't leave you
flailing; I'll shove a piece of cardboard

between your teeth, across the top
of your tongue
whether you like the taste or not.

You always seemed to sit
in front of me in class, like an epigraph,
sullen, half-drugged perhaps,

until your arms began to wave
as though excited to answer the only question
you'd try that day: Where am I?

And I, sitting so close,
always heard the answer,
trying not to fear those strange epiphanies

before the nun would sail down on us,
hold you till the resolution
and wipe your chin.

I think I understand now how things
seemed to catch up with you,
beyond sentence diagrams on the blackboard

and the grammar the rest of us were bound to.
Sometimes you'd just have to shake and groan
as though God were searching your parts

for a demon; and the nun, I really believe,
considered marking you absent
rather than admit her class was possessed

or that any of us could so easily
lose control, too far from those who might
hold on to our shaking shoulders.

SECOND TRIP TO AMHERST

at Emily Dickinson's grave

In between I told another poet
I'd visited this grave the first time,
alone on a foggy afternoon, my shoes
sinking in the sod.

I felt guilty, not for lying—
in fact I had turned in this direction,
felt the chill of the surrounding hills,

but now I've come up all the way
to the wrought-iron fence; there *is* fog,
some other stones overturned,
an empty Schlitz bottle in the path,

and I think of someone partying here
in this "Island of dishonored grass—"
all the society you could never stand,

and this—this plastic wreath
with plastic holly berries secured
with a twist tie to the fence
in this unnaturally warm January.

Almost the plausibility induces my belief—
I try to pick a plastic berry but it won't
come loose, a red and green mistake—

there, among three other Dickinsons,
all of whom have "died" while you,
I see from your stone, were "called back,"
snow burns off to "Kingdoms afterward"?

You never were quite sure.
Enough, I think, to document your stay.
You leave with less a lie that way.

About the Author

Robert Stewart has won a National Magazine Award for editorial achievement from the American Society of Magazine Editors. His poems have appeared in many literary journals, anthologies, and textbooks. Books include *The Narrow Gate: Writing, Art & Values* (essays, Serving House Books, 2014), *Outside Language: Essays* (Helicon Nine Editions, a finalist in the PEN Center USA Literary Awards for 2004; and winner of the Thorpe Menn Award); in addition to *Plumbers*, he has published the poetry chapbooks *Taking Leave, Rescue Mission, Climatron,* and a 2015 chapbook of poems, *Chickenhood*. He has directed the Midwest Poets Series on behalf of Rockhurst University in Kansas City since founding the series in 1983. He is editor of *New Letters* magazine and *New Letters on the Air*, a nationally syndicated literary radio program at the University of Missouri-Kansas City, where he also teaches in the Master of Fine Arts Program in Creative Writing and Media Arts.

About the Book

This book was composed in Trump Mediaeval, a typeface created by the German type designer Georg Trump in 1954. The original hardback was set, with design consultation, by Michael Annis Typography. The original jacket design, by Jane Weeks, has been adapted for the paperback edition by Cynthia Beard. The author would like to thank the late Conger Beasley Jr. for his editorial assistance on the first edition.

Pictured on the cover, circa 1949: a plumber named Louis H. Elmendorf, a member of St. Louis Journeymen Plumbers Local Union 35 (now Local 562), whose apprentice at the time was the author's father. The background, to the west, shows the roofline of the St. Louis Arena, which stood off of Oakland Avenue, across from Forest Park, from 1929–1999.